FAVOR & BLESSINGS JOURNAL

PRAY!

A 30-day Devotional Book to Change Your Mindset

OVERCOME INSECURITY & LACK

JOE JOE DAWSON
Kingdom Mindset Mentor

Pray! Favor and Blessings Journal: A 30-Day Devotional to Change Your Mindset and Overcome Insecurity and Lack

Copyright © 2024 by Joe Joe Dawson. All rights reserved. No part of this publication may be reproduced, distributed, or transmitted in any form or by any means, including photocopying, recording, or other electronic or mechanical methods, without the prior written permission of the copyright owner.

Contact Editor for permissions: joejoedawson@hotmail.com

Scriptures marked NKJV are taken from the NEW KING JAMES VERSION (NKJV): Scripture taken from the NEW KING JAMES VERSION®. Copyright© 1982 by Thomas Nelson, Inc. Used by permission. All rights reserved

Scriptures marked NLT are taken from the HOLY BIBLE, NEW LIVING TRANSLATION (NLT): Scriptures taken from the HOLY BIBLE, NEW LIVING TRANSLATION, Copyright© 1996, 2004, 2007 by Tyndale House Foundation. Used by permission of Tyndale House Publishers, Inc., Carol Stream, Illinois 60188. All rights reserved. Used by permission.

Scriptures marked NIV are taken from the NEW INTERNATIONAL VERSION (NIV): Scripture taken from THE HOLY BIBLE, NEW INTERNATIONAL VERSION ®. Copyright© 1973, 1978, 1984, 2011 by Biblica, Inc.™. Used by permission of Zondervan

All Scripture quotations are from The Passion Translation®. Copyright © 2017, 2018, 2020 by Passion & Fire Ministries, Inc. Used by permission. All rights reserved. ThePassionTranslation.com.

Scriptures marked AMP are taken from the AMPLIFIED BIBLE (AMP): Scripture taken from the AMPLIFIED® BIBLE, Copyright © 1954, 1958, 1962, 1964, 1965, 1987 by the Lockman Foundation Used by Permission. (www.Lockman.org)

Scriptures marked ESV are taken from the THE HOLY BIBLE, ENGLISH STANDARD VERSION (ESV): Scriptures taken from THE HOLY BIBLE, ENGLISH STANDARD VERSION ® Copyright© 2001 by Crossway, a publishing ministry of Good News Publishers. Used by permission.

www.joejoedawson.net

Note from the Author

I want to share with you my heart behind this new series of prayer journal devotional books. I don't know about you, but I absolutely love it when a pastor does a four-week series! He is able to dive deep into the Word and help his congregation study and understand a particular topic from many different angles. I've created this series of 30-day Devotional Books for the same reason.

I truly believe that if you can immerse yourself into a specific subject for a month, you'll receive a much fuller revelation of what the Word of God and the Spirit of the Lord are saying.

In each book, I'll provide you with a Focus Verse of the Day to start your devotional time. Then, I'll speak to you in a small devotion to help you understand the topic and show you how to apply it. Finally, I've written a guided prayer and a powerful declaration or two to show you how you can "pray and say" the truths of God's Word over your own life.

By engaging in this process, you'll develop a better mindset regarding the topic we're studying and gain deeper insights into God's perspective and how His Kingdom operates!

There is a noticeable lack of Christian education today, and many people, young and old alike, struggle to understand the Word of God, the Spirit of God, or the Kingdom of God. My aim is to address this issue...beginning with this prayer journal and devotional book series!

I invite you to join me on this remarkable 30-day journey through God's Word as we explore God's Favor and Blessings! It will change your thinking and propel you forward, empowering you to fulfill the Kingdom assignment on your life!

For His Kingdom,

Joe Joe Dawson

Joe Joe Dawson

Do You Need Prayer?

If you would like prayer for anything,
just click the Contact Button on our website.

JoeJoeDawson.net

I would love to pray with you.

DAY 1

Focus Verse of the Day

And my God shall supply all your need according to His riches in glory by Christ Jesus.
Philippians 4:19 NKJV

Devotion

I'm so grateful that my God has more than enough to care for all my needs. He has such a generous heart and wants to see His kids covered in every area of their lives. His endless supplies will never run out. We must recognize that we aren't blessed because WE are good; it's because HE is good and has shown us extreme favor. The Father's heart toward us is to love and care for us. He gives us what we need and want according to our maturity. That's true love, to see us grow up into Him.

Gratitude

_____
_____
_____

_____/_____/_____

Reflection

_____
_____
_____
_____
_____
_____
_____
_____
_____
_____
_____

Prayer

Father, I thank You that You have more than enough to provide for my needs. Your surplus is so vast it is beyond my comprehension. You will take care of every one of my needs, wants, and desires because You are a good Father, and You delight in meeting all of Your children's needs. I'll focus on You and doing Your will, and I won't worry about my own needs because You're my loving, heavenly Father, and I know You've got me completely taken care of. Amen.

DAY 2

Focus Verse of the Day

When you open your generous hand,
it's full of blessings, satisfying
the longings of every living thing.
Psalms 145:16 TPT

Devotion

When we seek God's face, we get the hand of blessing. We were created for fellowship with Him. Many people seek Him because they have a want or a need, but they forget the intimate relationship that the Lord desires from us. That's what He wants with us. There's no greater feeling than knowing that you are in the perfect will of God. That's where blessings flow. That's where we have peace that surpasses all understanding. We know God through a deep personal relationship. Like a good father, He showers us with loving kindness and favor.

Gratitude

_____
_____
_____

_____/_____/_____

Reflection

_____
_____
_____
_____
_____
_____
_____
_____
_____
_____

Prayer

Father, I thank you so much for your generous hand today. Thank you for all of the abundant blessings that flow from there. I pray that I can share and steward every blessing I've ever had that came from you. Father, guide me and lead me today, and just as you have blessed me, I pray that I'm a blessing to other people. Amen.

DAY 3

Focus Verse of the Day

Let the favor of the Lord our God be upon us, and establish the work of our hands upon us; yes, establish the work of our hands!
Psalm 90:17 ESV

Devotion

When we walk close to God, we receive His favor and blessings. The more we know His heart, the more we understand our calling and can carry out our Kingdom assignments with extravagant favor from Him. He will bless the works of our hands, and we will succeed in whatever we do with an abundant anointing. The Holy Spirit will guide us and move us into proper alignment with the plans of Heaven for our lives.

Gratitude

_____
_____
_____

_____/_____/_____

Reflection

_____
_____
_____
_____
_____
_____
_____
_____
_____
_____
_____

Prayer

Father, today I declare that as You favor me and put Your abundant blessing on my life and upon all that I do, I will fully receive everything You have for me. And then I will turn around and show the favor of the Lord to other people, and then they will turn around and do the same thing! You'll bless me, then I'll bless others, and then they'll be a blessing, too! So, Lord, I pray that Your favor rains down on me and flows to every person I come in contact with today. Amen.

DAY 4

Focus Verse of the Day

Every good gift and every perfect gift is from above, and comes down from the Father of lights, with whom there is no variation or shadow of turning.
James 1:17 NKJV

Devotion

We should always thank God for every gift and blessing that comes our way. No matter how big or small or how it manifests to us, give God all the glory. God knows when our heart is ready to receive certain blessings. We should have an extreme heart of gratitude toward the Lord for watching over us and bringing the right people and gifts to us at the right time. Our great heavenly Father always watches out for us. His timing is completely perfect!

Gratitude

_____
_____
_____

_____/_____/_____

Reflection

_____
_____
_____
_____
_____
_____
_____
_____
_____
_____

Prayer

God, I thank You for every single gift and blessing that is coming my way this week. It doesn't matter where they come from, I know that ultimately, they came from You. Lord, I pray that I receive these blessings and these gifts in such abundance that there is such an overflow that every person around me is blessed because of them. Thank You for Your loving kindness and Your faithful provision. Amen.

DAY 5

Focus Verse of the Day

And the child Samuel grew in stature,
and in favor both with the Lord and men.
1 Samuel 2:26 NKJV

Devotion

Just like Samuel, if we follow God's voice, He will guide us and lead us in all the ways of His Kingdom. God has so many amazing adventures to take us on if we will just listen and move in the direction He tells us to go. The Lord has divine relations and phenomenal doors that only the favor of God can open. The Lord will put us in rooms that we never dreamed of being in and give us opportunities that will surprise everyone. Listening and obeying God's voice will change your life, and His blessing will make things work out in your favor.

Gratitude

_____
_____
_____

_____/_____/_____

Reflection

_____
_____
_____
_____
_____
_____
_____
_____
_____
_____

Prayer

Dear Lord, I pray that today I'll grow in the stature of the Kingdom of God, that I'll be in right standing with You, and that I'll have a Kingdom mindset. As You pour out Your favor upon my life, I'll walk humbly and steward this favor and power properly. I thank You that I'll have both Your favor and the favor of man upon my life this week, and I declare that I'm going to impact a lot of people for the Kingdom of God! Amen.

DAY 6

Focus Verse of the Day

For You, O Lord, will bless the righteous; With favor You will surround him as with a shield.
Psalm 5:12 NKJV

Devotion

God always shows kindness and favor toward the ones who walk in righteousness and stand up for what is right in His sight. The Lord will show up as a strong tower and refuge for those willing to be bold for the sake of the Gospel of Jesus Christ. When the enemy comes toward us, the armies of the Lord will protect us as a shield from the enemy and his plans. God is a faithful and protective Father who always has our best interest at heart.

Gratitude

_____
_____
_____

_____/_____/_____

Reflection

_____
_____
_____
_____
_____
_____
_____
_____
_____
_____
_____

Prayer

Father, I declare that Your favor will flow over me now and overtake me as a protective guard around me. As I move toward You into righteousness, I know that You will bless me as I go about my day, and I will make a Kingdom impact on every person I come into contact with! I declare that You order my steps, and together we have a blessed day and further the mission of the Kingdom! Amen.

DAY 7

Focus Verse of the Day

Blessed be the God and Father of our Lord Jesus Christ, who has blessed us with every spiritual blessing in the heavenly places in Christ.
Ephesians 1:3 NKJV

Devotion

Never for one minute of your life think that God isn't good; He is the absolute best! Since our Heavenly Father has no lack, we don't either. Sometimes our limited thinking hinders us, but with Kingdom thinking, we understand that we can walk in the fullness of blessing that God intends for us to have. Always remember there is no limit to the Kingdom of God, so we should have no limit. You are so blessed, so walk as a child of God!

Gratitude

_____
_____
_____

_____/_____/_____

Reflection

_____
_____
_____
_____
_____
_____
_____
_____
_____
_____

Prayer

Today, Lord, I want to thank You for the many spiritual blessings that You have given us. I thank You for Your favor as we go out and activate the Kingdom of God in every area that we step into. And Lord, I pray that today we have the eyes of Christ to see every person who needs what we have, which is the hope that You have given us. I pray that we adjust our focus and our mindset so that we're able to carry these blessings and favor to every person that we encounter today! Amen.

DAY 8

Focus Verse of the Day

For the Lord God is a sun and shield;
The Lord will give grace and glory;
No good thing will He withhold
From those who walk uprightly.
Psalm 84:11 NKJV

Devotion

It's such an amazing feeling to know that my God has me covered in every area of my life. He is not a stingy Father who keeps things from us but a good Father who loves to shower us with extreme favor and radical blessings! The Lord gives us glorious grace that extends further than we could ever imagine. His protection over us is at a Kingdom level that surpasses our earthly knowledge. His love is off the charts for His kids who walk in holiness and righteousness.

Gratitude

_____
_____
_____

_____/_____/_____

Reflection

_____
_____
_____
_____
_____
_____
_____
_____
_____
_____

Prayer

Lord, today, I pray that I'll carry Your grace and Your glory with dignity and honor. I pray that as I cultivate a stronger, personal relationship with You, I'll understand every good thing that You have destined for me. I pray that I won't speak word curses over myself or block any blessing that You have for me, but that I'll receive them and walk in them. I'll take every blessing that You have for me because the more blessings I walk in, the more I can give to others! Amen.

DAY 9

Focus Verse of the Day

The blessing of the Lord makes one rich,
And He adds no sorrow with it.
Proverbs 10:22 NKJV

Devotion

We should always have a heart of gratitude toward God's many blessings. The Lord can add to our lives in a smooth way without repercussion or trouble. When we walk uprightly with the Lord and carry the wisdom as Solomon did, we can have an easier life than if we went the ways of the world. Many people try to have success in life without God or even try to force things. They never turn out as good as when we follow the leading of the Lord through the Holy Spirit. Where the Spirit leads, peace will follow.

Gratitude

_____

_____

_____

____/____/____

Reflection

_____
_____
_____
_____
_____
_____
_____
_____
_____
_____
_____
_____

Prayer

Father, today I pray that I understand the difference between the wealth and riches of the Kingdom of God and those of earthly avenues. I pray that as I hold tightly to a Kingdom mindset, I will fulfill everything that You have for me. I pray that I am a blessing to each and every person that comes into contact with me. And Lord, I pray that I will never seek riches in any way that is not pleasing to You. I declare that my eyes and my heart will always be with You! Amen.

DAY 10

Focus Verse of the Day

Yes, God is more than ready to overwhelm you with every form of grace, so that you will have more than enough of everything—every moment and in every way. He will make you overflow with abundance in every good thing you do.
2 Corinthians 9:8 TPT

Devotion

My God has a surplus of everything we could ever need. It doesn't matter if it's more peace, joy, healing, miracles, friends, or mindset upgrade, God's got you covered. He is willing to put the right people and situations around you to help you accomplish your Kingdom assignment. In whatever season of life you're in, His grace and power are available. If you find yourself in a circumstance that you don't know how to navigate, God will guide you. He will overwhelm you with His superabundant favor and blessings.

Gratitude

_____
_____
_____

_____/_____/_____

Reflection

_____
_____
_____
_____
_____
_____
_____
_____
_____
_____
_____

Prayer

Today, Lord, I pray that as You overwhelm me with Your amazing goodness, I will always walk in humility. I will move forward in life with more than enough, and I will bless every person who comes in contact with me. I thank You that in every moment of my life, in everything I do, I will have abundance, and I will walk in overflow for the Kingdom of God. I will never lack because I am with You. And Lord, I pray that as I am blessed, I will become a blessing to others. Amen.

DAY 11

Focus Verse of the Day

And from the overflow of his fullness we received grace heaped upon more grace!
John 1:16 TPT

Devotion

God wants us to walk in the absolute fullness of His anointing, which will overflow into every area of our lives. He gives us grace to carry out His mission and a strong anointing for whatever He has put in our hearts and hands to do. Never put too much pressure on yourself, thinking you have to do everything in your natural ability. That's why we have the great gift of the grace of God! The Lord will anoint you and bless your best efforts to the place where you will overflow to everyone around you. And that is how the message of the gospel will go forth!

Gratitude

_____
_____
_____

_____/_____/_____

Reflection

_____
_____
_____
_____
_____
_____
_____
_____
_____
_____

Prayer

Father, I pray I get closer and closer to You as I walk in all the fullness of the Kingdom of God each day. I declare that as I overflow with Your favor and blessing, I'll become a huge blessing to every person I meet. When people come in contact with me, they'll sense that the fullness of God can also be their portion. By the Presence of God that dwells upon my life, every person I meet will want You more and more until their life overflows with total abundance. Amen.

DAY 12

Focus Verse of the Day

> Oh, taste and see that the Lord is good!
> Blessed is the man who takes refuge in him!
> Psalm 34:8 ESV

Devotion

As we go through different trials and tests, remember that God offers us so much grace. Because of this grace, we can and will get through every situation and circumstance. We will have an overflow of God's goodness at our side as we carry out our Kingdom purpose without wavering. Whenever life gets difficult, remember that more grace is available to be poured out to you. Your life is supposed to be an example for the Kingdom, and we are in a covenant with God to walk in the overflow of His goodness.

Gratitude

_____
_____
_____

_____/_____/_____

Reflection

_____
_____
_____
_____
_____
_____
_____
_____
_____
_____
_____
_____

Prayer

Father, I pray that I will always run to You, for You are my strength! I declare that in every aspect and situation of my life, I will see the goodness of God. I pray that every day, I will run to You and draw closer to You, and I will never look for satisfaction anywhere but in the very middle of the Presence of God. Today, I pray that I will receive "downloads" from Heaven to walk in a greater revelation of the Kingdom of God! Amen.

DAY 13

Focus Verse of the Day

> For whoever finds me finds life,
> And obtains favor from the Lord;
> Proverbs 8:35 NKJV

Devotion

Wisdom is the beginning of living a blessed life with God. Why do people consider Solomon to be so wise? Because he asked for wisdom above anything else! When you walk in godly wisdom, you will make Kingdom-minded decisions and the right choices in life. Many people lack what they need because they don't walk in the wisdom of the Lord. The Word says if you want wisdom, ask for it. God wants you and me to walk in wisdom. Let's all ask for daily wisdom to carry out our God-given assignments.

Gratitude

_____
_____
_____

_____/_____/_____

Reflection

Prayer

Lord, I declare that I will run hard after You every day. Each day, I will live more and more in the favor of God. Your abundance of blessings will flow and be evident in my life, causing people to want to encounter and see the goodness of God in their own lives. And Lord, I pray that You will give me strength to pursue You in everything I do! Amen.

DAY 14

Focus Verse of the Day

The Lord bless you and keep you;
The Lord make His face shine upon you,
And be gracious to you.
Numbers 6:24-25 NKJV

Devotion

When a father looks at his children and speaks blessings over them, it's a spiritual act and an emotional boost for the kids. Everyone needs affirmation from their natural parents, grandparents, spiritual parents, and mentors. It's good when people are blessed by those in authority over them. But when God Almighty speaks over us, WOW! Everything shifts when we hear from Him. Fear and insecurity leave, and the promises and prophetic words start to manifest. Life changes in that moment.

Gratitude

_____
_____
_____

_____/_____/_____

Reflection

_____
_____
_____
_____
_____
_____
_____
_____
_____
_____

Prayer

Father, I pray that through all the days of my life, I will walk in Your amazing favor and blessing. Lord, I pray that You will be with me and keep me from moving to the right or the left so I will always keep my focus and gaze upon You. Therefore, Your face will always shine upon me, and I will walk in everything that the Kingdom of God has for me. Lord, I pray that my life will be an example for others to follow. Amen.

DAY 15

Focus Verse of the Day

And the peace of God, which surpasses all understanding, will guard your hearts and minds through Christ Jesus.
Philippians 4:7 NKJV

Devotion

Guard your mind! Your mindset determines everything. When we have a Kingdom mindset, we see things according to the scripture and Heaven. The peace of God is needed to think clearly. It gives us the godly clarity to steward our lives properly. When our mind is healthy, we make the best possible decisions every time. Therefore, we don't have to waste valuable time backtracking to undo wrong decisions. Think Kingdom and think forward. The favor of God will rest on a sound mind.

Gratitude

_____
_____
_____

_____/_____/_____

Reflection

_____
_____
_____
_____
_____
_____
_____
_____
_____
_____
_____

Prayer

Father, I pray I will always follow Your peace in every situation and circumstance. Fear and insecurity will go as the understanding and wisdom of God triumph over them every time! Lord, I pray that my heart and mind will be at ease and in total peace in every situation throughout life. I declare that an abundance of blessing and favor will be my portion so that my life can be an example of the Kingdom of God as I walk out the path you have paved for me.

DAY 16

Focus Verse of the Day

Now to Him who is able to [carry out His purpose and] do superabundantly more than all that we dare ask or think [infinitely beyond our greatest prayers, hopes, or dreams], according to His power that is at work within us.
Ephesians 3:20 AMP

Devotion

The Lord wants you to be heavily blessed and walk in His weighty favor. This scripture challenges us to dream big, think colossal-sized thoughts, ask enormously, hope extravagantly, and pray wild prayers. God wants to do supernatural things in us and for us. He calls out to the Wild Ones who will do great exploits with Him and for Him. The Lord offers a life full of blessings if we just receive it. Live your God-centered life with no limits or restraints. Let's go!

Gratitude

_____
_____
_____

_____/_____/_____

Reflection

Prayer

Father, thank You so much for Your extreme favor as You pour out Your blessings upon us. Thank You, Lord, for multiplying our prayers and doing more than we could ever hope, dream, or pray about. Even beyond our wildest imaginations and thoughts, You will multiply what we pray for because You have more in store for us than we could ever imagine. Today, we want to thank You for being a great Father! Amen.

DAY 17

Focus Verse of the Day

What joy overwhelms everyone who keeps the ways of God, those who seek him as their heart's passion!
Psalm 119:2 TPT

Devotion

When you find a person full of the joy of the Lord, you find a blessed person. You find a person who puts their trust in the Lord. God always blesses the individual who seeks Him wholeheartedly. When you seek Him with your whole heart, you will find Him and His extravagant favor. The word 'heart' is broken into three parts: spirit, mind, and emotions. We must seek Him with all three. People with overflowing joy are strong in their spirits, minds, and emotions.

Gratitude

_____
_____
_____

_____/_____/_____

Reflection

_____
_____
_____
_____
_____
_____
_____
_____
_____
_____

Prayer

Father, I pray that I will diligently seek You with all of my heart all the days of my life. I pray that I will keep my focus on the assignments You've called me to and walk side by side and step by step with You as I fulfill my destiny. Lord, I pray that throughout my life, my heart will stay hungry and thirsty for the things You have for me as I focus on Your desires for my life and not my own. Amen.

DAY 18

Focus Verse of the Day

But seek first the kingdom of God
and His righteousness,
and all these things shall be added to you.
Matthew 6:33 NKJV

Devotion

When we seek the Kingdom, we tap into God's plans and agenda for Heaven to invade Earth. God has a plan for His will to be accomplished and His righteousness to flourish on the Earth. When we aggressively pursue Him and His purpose, we partner with Heaven. The Bible says He will take care of our needs and desires. God knows our hearts, and when He sees that we are focused on Him, He can't help but bless us and pour out His favor all over our lives!

Gratitude

_____
_____
_____

_____/_____/_____

Reflection

_____
_____
_____
_____
_____
_____
_____
_____
_____
_____
_____
_____

Prayer

Father, I pray that I keep the Kingdom of God as my number one priority. Lord, I pray that I have the heart of Christ in everything I do, always putting the Kingdom's needs and desires before my own. I pray that as I seek You on a daily basis, I grow closer to You in a personal relationship. I declare that I will fulfill the destiny that You have laid out for me as I manifest my Kingdom assignment on Earth. Amen.

DAY 19

Focus Verse of the Day

For I know the thoughts that I think toward you, says the Lord, thoughts of peace and not of evil, to give you a future and a hope.
Jeremiah 29:11 NKJV

Devotion

Think about it: the King of the Universe is thinking about you. He only has good plans for you, so fear and insecurities must go. When we partner with the thoughts Heaven has for us, we start to walk in abundance and operate from an unshakable Kingdom. Knowing the Lord has a breathtaking purpose for me fires me up! I wake up and start each day with loud gratitude to my Jesus because He only thinks about my bright future with Him. He loves us so much and has a life-altering purpose for us. Walk in it!

Gratitude

_____

_____

_____

___/___/___

Reflection

Prayer

Lord, I thank You so much for being amazingly good to me! Thank you for always having my best interests in Your heart and mind. I pray that I will never walk in the spirit of fear but always keep my eyes focused on what You have for me. You've given every one of us a breathtaking purpose to fulfill on this Earth. Thank You for entrusting us with this Kingdom destiny so we can help change the world for You! Amen.

DAY 20

Focus Verse of the Day

Whoever gives heed to instruction prospers, and blessed is the one who trusts in the Lord.
Proverbs 16:20 NIV

Devotion

God will always guide you by the Holy Spirit. If we learn to lean into the wisdom and understanding of the Lord, we will prosper in life and in everything He has called us to do. Many people feel unfulfilled because they simply don't get their instructions from the Lord or navigate life with those instructions. His ways are higher than ours, plus life flows with favor when you are in the center of His will. If you don't feel like you're in His perfect will, get there as fast as possible. There is a flow to life, and His protection is refreshing and satisfying.

Gratitude

_____

_____

_____

_____/_____/_____

Reflection

_____
_____
_____
_____
_____
_____
_____
_____
_____
_____
_____

Prayer

Father, I pray that I will always listen to the instructions You give me through the written Word, the prophetic word, and wise teaching. I pray to consistently put my hope, faith, and trust in You. Thank You, Lord, for blessing me with every good and perfect blessing from above. I pray for a strong relationship with You all the days of my life. I will prosper because I will listen to all the instructions that You give me. Amen.

DAY 21

Focus Verse of the Day

Blessed is the man who trusts in the Lord,
And whose hope is the Lord.
Jeremiah 17:7 NKJV

Devotion

Blessed is the man devoted to the Lord, no matter the situation. The one who trusts in the written Word of God will be able to withstand any trial or test and come out blessed on the other side. My hope for complete deliverance in any circumstance is 100% based on the Lord and how He helps me to think through the process. I put my faith in the Lord without reservation and pray that the Holy Spirit guides me to handle the aftermath properly. God wants us to have good character and to represent Him at all times.

Gratitude

_____

_____

_____

_____/_____/_____

Reflection

_____
_____
_____
_____
_____
_____
_____
_____
_____
_____

Prayer

Father, I want to thank You for being so trustworthy. Thank You for always being in my corner and always believing in me. Thank you for always pulling and pushing me through every situation by the power of the Holy Spirit. Thank You for blessing me and putting Your favor upon me to accomplish my God assignment. Thank You, Lord, for giving me so much hope. I pray that I will always keep my eyes on You because You are where my hope and my help come from! Amen.

DAY 22

Focus Verse of the Day

Lord, how wonderful you are! You have stored up so many good things for us, like a treasure chest heaped up and spilling over with blessings—all for those who honor and worship you! Everybody knows what you can do for those who turn and hide themselves in you.
Psalm 31:19 TPT

Devotion

The Lord has more blessings than you could ever imagine—He's just waiting on you to get yourself in a position where you can accept them. When you tap into His overflowing favor, God will pour out His wisdom and treasures in a measure you can't even contain. The Father wants people to lose themselves in His presence and walk in the Spirit in an unfathomable abundance. As a Kingdom citizen, wisdom, knowledge, and understanding are your portion.

Gratitude

_____

_____

_____

_____/_____/_____

Reflection

_____
_____
_____
_____
_____
_____
_____
_____
_____
_____

Prayer

Lord, I pray I will always keep myself 100% hidden in Christ. I thank You for the many blessings You have poured upon us, to the point that they overflow. Thank You for the favor we have with both You and man. All the days of our lives, we will be blessed and a blessing to every person who comes in contact with us. I speak life over every person I interact with today because I'm walking in the favor of God! Amen.

DAY 23

Focus Verse of the Day

Before you do anything,
put your trust totally in God and not in yourself.
Then every plan you make will succeed.
Proverbs 4:16 TPT

Devotion

God wants us to roll all our concerns and cares onto Him so we can concentrate on building the God-dream He gave us. When you build a foundation on God, that foundation can carry the weight of any structure. In life, we need God to carry the pressure of life and the unforseen obstacles that pop up from time to time. Success in anything is in how you start the process and who you start it with. Placing God as the main priority in anything means you have a better chance of succeeding.

Gratitude

_____
_____
_____

_____/_____/_____

Reflection

Prayer

Father, I pray that I throw my life completely into Your will and embrace the perfect plan You have for me! I also pray that I will never rely on my own gifts, talents, or abilities but will always yield to the leading of the Holy Spirit. Thank You for Your promises that assure I will thrive in everything I do, be blessed, and walk in the abundant favor of God. I pray that I will walk in both extreme power and extreme humility. Thank You for blessing me with the life that I am living. Amen.

DAY 24

Focus Verse of the Day

> May he grant you your heart's desire
> and fulfill all your plans!
> Psalm 20:4 ESV

Devotion

My daily prayer is that God will place His dreams and desires in my heart so that I can carry them out for Him. When I go about my day, I will walk in favor because I'm accomplishing Heaven's plan and agenda. When we die to the flesh daily, we will consistently live in the Spirit. As we do, our constant daily walk builds traction, and we make progress on our plans until they are complete. A person who follows the Lord on a daily basis has continual favor. Get into the flow and walk in blessings!

Gratitude

_____
_____
_____

____/____/____

Reflection

_____
_____
_____
_____
_____
_____
_____
_____
_____
_____
_____

Prayer

Lord, I pray that You'll put Your desires in my heart so that I may carry out Your desires. I pray that the Kingdom of God will be manifested through my life every single day. I pray I will never put my wants and needs before those of the Kingdom. I pray I will become a better servant for You each day. If You need something done on the Earth, I pray that You will consider me worthy to give me that prophetic word so I can carry it out. Amen.

DAY 25

Focus Verse of the Day

Blessed are those who hunger and thirst for righteousness, For they shall be filled.
Matthew 5:6 NKJV

Devotion

When you pray to remain hungry and thirsty for the Lord, you will gain a more robust appetite for the Word and prayer. You search for something to satisfy you when you're hungry and thirsty, but the Lord is the only thing that can satisfy a true believer. Nothing in the natural world can quench our thirst for God alone. No amount of natural substance can fill our spiritual hunger besides the Lord Himself. My God is more than enough.

Gratitude

_____

_____

_____

____/____/____

Reflection

Prayer

Father, I pray to be filled with Your Spirit to the point of overflowing. God, may all the days of my life be marked by a hunger for Your Presence and a thirst for everything the Holy Spirit has for me. Lord, I want to walk in holiness and righteousness each day. I pray to be consumed with You—Your Presence, Your Power, and everything Heaven offers. I declare that I will always walk in the ways You have set before me. Amen.

DAY 26

Focus Verse of the Day

A good name is to be chosen
rather than great riches,
Loving favor rather than silver and gold.
Proverbs 22:1 NKJV

Devotion

The Lord sends each person to earth with an amazing purpose, but many lose sight of their God-calling and destiny and start chasing gold and silver instead. The Lord wants us to keep a good name and avoid being consumed with the things of this world. His desire is for us to be blessed but not by the ways of the world. If we follow the Lord's guidance, things will work out really well, but usually, there is no model to follow. Instead of following a worldly example, the Holy Spirit is your only true guide.

Gratitude

_____
_____
_____

_____/_____/_____

Reflection

_____
_____
_____
_____
_____
_____
_____
_____
_____
_____
_____

Prayer

Father, I declare that I will walk uprightly before You. I pray that all the days of my life, I will seek Your face and not the approval or riches of man. Lord, I declare that today and every day, I will follow after the leading of the Holy Spirit, doing everything that You have called me to do. I declare that I will do no person wrong but will always walk as a great example for Jesus Christ. Amen.

DAY 27

Focus Verse of the Day

Now may God, the fountain of hope, fill you to overflowing with uncontainable joy and perfect peace as you trust in him. And may the power of the Holy Spirit continually surround your life with his super-abundance until you radiate with hope!
Romans 15:13 TPT

Devotion

When we partner with the powerful Holy Spirit, everything changes. Your foundation becomes solid, and your life flows like a well-oiled machine. Things begin to align themselves by the Spirit. When you overflow with God, the levels of your anointing also start to rise. You will see better opportunities suddenly appear, and amazing new doors will open automatically for you. Your joy and hope will go off the charts. The favor of God takes everything up to the next level—the level of the Kingdom of God.

Gratitude

_____
_____
_____

_____/_____/_____

Reflection

_____
_____
_____
_____
_____
_____
_____
_____
_____
_____
_____

Prayer

Father, I pray that my love, joy, and peace from the Holy Spirit overflow to a degree that I cannot contain myself today. As I walk in the radical favor of God, I declare that every person I come in contact with will be blessed! I pray that the Holy Spirit guides and leads me, and I will walk in the abundance of the Lord. I thank You for blessing me with every blessing available from Heaven. And Father, I declare today that I am a witness who will share the love and joy of Christ with many!

DAY 28

Focus Verse of the Day

He who dwells in the secret place of the Most High
Shall abide under the shadow of the Almighty.
I will say of the Lord, 'He is my refuge and my fortress; My God, in Him I will trust.'
Psalms 91:1-2 NKJV

Devotion

If we dwell in the private secret place with God, our daily communication with Him will place our soul and spirit safely under His protection. The presence of God offers us unspeakable comfort and serenity that you will never find on Earth without knowing Him. When we trust the Lord, He will bring us success that can only be achieved by accessing the Kingdom of God. Earthly fulfillment leaves you empty when compared to the Kingdom.

Gratitude

_____

_____

_____

___/___/___

Reflection

_____
_____
_____
_____
_____
_____
_____
_____
_____
_____

Prayer

Father, I thank You for being a safe and strong tower I can always run to and take refuge in. Today, Lord, I pray that Your love will shower over me like a canopy of extreme favor and blessing. I thank You that I can always look to You to give me peace, counsel, and power in any situation and circumstance. Thank You for always being my faithful Father. Amen.

DAY 29

Focus Verse of the Day

> Blessed are the pure in heart,
> For they shall see God.
> Matthew 5:8 NKJV

Devotion

Whenever you become pure-hearted with the Lord, you will begin to walk in a combination of holiness, peace, and joy. You can live a life where you are truly happy and walk in the abundance of every good thing. There is no limit to what you can achieve on this Earth when walking close to God. Our souls were made to prosper and be at total peace with Him. Our minds are supposed to be sound and creative. Purity is a place where our spirit, soul, and body are truly consecrated to God.

Gratitude

_____
_____
_____

_____/_____/_____

Reflection

Prayer

Lord, thank You for always dealing with my heart in every aspect of my life. I pray that I will always have a pure heart toward You and the things of your Kingdom. I pray that in every situation, the Holy Spirit will guide me, lead me, comfort me, and correct me so that I will have a pure heart for Your people. Lord, I pray that You will direct me throughout this week and help me be a shining example of the pure love of God! Amen.

DAY 30

Focus Verse of the Day

Surely goodness and mercy shall follow me
All the days of my life;
And I will dwell in the house of the Lord
Forever.
Psalm 23:6 NKJV

Devotion

When you are truly set apart for the Lord and the Kingdom of God, you will begin to walk in the favor of God at a level that others will notice. People will see a huge difference in you because you have devoted your life to God. They'll notice that His goodness is your portion. When people ask, you give God all the glory and share your passionate faith. His mercy will wrap around you like a blanket and will be your protection and portion. You were created to walk with God all the days of your life.

Gratitude

_____

_____

_____

_____/_____/_____

Reflection

Prayer

Lord, thank You for offering me an amazing life here on Earth and in eternity. Thank You for blessing me with the assurance that Your goodness will always be with me, that mercy is my portion, and that Your favor will be upon me all the days of my life. Lord, I will continually seek Your face on a daily basis. Give me strength to carry out my God-calling so I will fulfill the Kingdom destiny placed on my life! Amen.

Bonus Content

Unprecedented Favor & Blessings

Recently, during a corporate prayer session, I heard this: unprecedented favor and blessings. Now, you might immediately say, "Woo! The favor of the Lord's upon me! The blessings of the Lord are coming my way!"

But I have a reminder for you.

Some people can't handle the favor and blessings of God when they come because they don't know how to steward them. Whenever God gives prophetic words or promises, He gives them to people who will care for them and who will have the ability to push them through.

God says there are unprecedented favors and blessings for you in a realm you can't even imagine—but YOU are going to have to steward them!

For example, He might bless you financially. What will you do with that blessing? Will you keep it all for yourself, or will you GIVE to others? There are so many ministries, nonprofits, charities, orphans, and widows out there.

Recently, a great friend of mine shared that he had a huge financial blessing come his way. He told me, "I just want to sow into an orphanage. James 1:27 talks about widows and orphans. I know some widows; I know some orphans. I want to bless them."

He didn't keep the blessing all for himself but used it to bless others. That's a Kingdom-minded person!

Many times, people who are experiencing a lot of needs in their lives need a mental breakthrough more than they need a financial or health breakthrough. It is their broken mindset that is keeping them from walking in the fullness of what God has for them.

Philippians 4:19 says, "I am convinced that my God will fully satisfy every need that you have, for I have seen the abundant riches of glory revealed to me through Jesus Christ" (TPT).

God has abundant riches and glory that He wants to bestow upon His kids. But when His kids aren't thinking properly, they hold themselves back from receiving what He has for them. It's not God hindering them; they are hindering themselves.

James 1:17 says, "Every good gift and every perfect gift is from above, and comes down from the Father of lights, with whom there is no variation or shadow of turning" (NKJV).

Recently, I gave someone a financial blessing. They said, "Thank you, Joe Joe!" I responded, "Hey, look, I'm not trying to be a super spiritual guy here, but I'm telling you, every good and perfect gift comes from the LORD."

Yes, the check had my name on it, but let me assure you, it was a gift from the Lord.

God has more for you than you could ever even imagine—gifts, talents, abilities, healings, finances, restoration, whatever you need! But so many people won't receive what He wants to give them.

We were at a conference recently, and the power of God was flowing. Prophetic ministry was flowing. Healing ministry was flowing.

I was praying for the people, and as I went down the line, one man stopped me and said, "Let me tell you my story."

I said, "Let me just prophesy and pray."

"You don't understand how bad I've had it," he responded.

I countered, "You don't understand how good my God is. Just let me pray."

He argued, "No, I really need to tell you my story. You need to know how bad my life has been the last few years."

"Do you see how many people are in this line?" I asked him. "Let me pray. Let me prophesy over you. Let me speak life over you."

"But I want to tell you how bad it's been."

I said, "You know what? I'm going to move on to the next person."

I never prayed for that person because all he wanted to do was complain about how bad things had been for him! He was so caught up in his mindset that he limited God.

You need to understand that you're not waiting on God—God's waiting on you! He's waiting for you to get your mindset into proper alignment so you can receive His blessings!

In John 1:15-16, John tells the people about Jesus, "This was he of whom I said, 'He who comes after me ranks before me, because he was before me.' For from his fullness we have all received, grace upon grace" (ESV).

From the overflow of HIS fullness, He gives us grace upon more grace. When the Holy Spirit moves on your life, favor upon favor, blessing upon blessing, grace upon grace are yours. Are you ready to receive them?

Recently, the Lord gave me a prophetic word, and then somebody called and gave me the exact same prophetic word.

They said, "Joe, you're about to walk in abundance upon abundance. You're about to walk in favor upon favor. You're about to walk in opportunity upon opportunity."

So, do you know what I did? I began fasting and praying even more that week because I wanted to make sure I was properly aligned with the Holy Spirit to receive everything that God had for me!

What are you doing to get ready to receive?

Second Corinthians 1:2 says, "May undeserved favor and endless peace be yours continually from our Father God and from our Lord Jesus, the Anointed One!" (TPT)

Wait a minute, what in the world did that scripture say?

Undeserved favor and endless peace?

We don't deserve it, but THAT is our portion!

My kids often get undeserved favor. Recently, I gave each one of them a little bit of extra money. It wasn't for any chores. I just wanted to do something special for them.

They asked me, "What's this for?"

I told them, "I don't know. I just saw y'all sitting there, and I wanted to bless you. You carry my last name, and I love you."

That's undeserved favor!

Endless peace is yours too!

Some of you don't have peace right now, but endless peace is available to you if you take it. I declare that the peace of God that passes all understanding is YOUR portion!

What do you say, friend?

Favor, blessings, and endless peace are yours!

Get ready to receive!

About the Author

Joe Joe Dawson, the Founder and Apostle of Roar Church Texarkana, is a visionary spiritual leader who is passionate about igniting awakening and revival.

As a transformative mindset mentor and bestselling author of influential books such as 'Kingdom Thinking' and 'Living Your God-Sized Dream,' Joe Joe empowers people to connect with God, shatter the limits of their thinking, and achieve supernatural success.

Beyond the pages of his books, Joe Joe reaches a broad audience through his popular YouTube show 'Joe Joe in the Morning,' where he offers daily encouragement and practical strategies for living 'your best life ever.' His down-to-earth manner and practical spirituality resonate with individuals from all walks of life.

Joe Joe is happily married to the love of his life, Autumn, and together they are raising three exceptional children - Malachi, Judah, and Ezra.

In addition to their ministry, this influential couple owns multiple businesses, including a thriving health coaching venture and the rapidly growing mentorship program, Mentored by Joe Joe Dawson.

Are you interested in mentoring?

For more information about our mentoring program, Mentored by Joe Joe Dawson, visit our website:

JoeJoeDawson.net

Did the

Favor & Blessings Journal

help you?

If so, please leave an honest review
so others can be helped by it too!

Thank you!

Connect with Joe Joe Dawson

JOE JOE DAWSON
Facebook

@JOE_JOE_DAWSONTXK
Instagram

@JoeJoeDawson
YouTube

@PASTORJOEDAWSON
Twitter

JoeJoeDawson
Rumble

JOEJOEDAWSON.NET
Website

Other Books by the Author

Build Create Design
Kingdom Thinking
Personal Turnaround
The 40 P's of the Apostolic
Living Your God-Sized Dream
Recipe for Revival
Unworthy But Called
Kingdom Mindset
The Flow
Fast Track
Moving Forward
Voices of Roar
Destiny Dimensions

Made in the USA
Monee, IL
29 May 2024